LANGSTON HUGHES

Brigid Gallagher

Heinemann
LIBRARY

Chicago, Illinois

www.capstonepub.com
Visit our website to find out more information about Heinemann-Raintree books.

To order:
☎ Phone 800-747-4992
🖥 Visit www.capstonepub.com to browse our catalog and order online.

© 2013 Heinemann Library
An imprint of Capstone Global Library, LLC
Chicago, Illinois

Edited by Abby Colich, Megan Cotugno, and Laura Hensley
Designed by Philippa Jenkins
Original illustrations © Capstone Global Library Limited 2011
Illustrated by Oxford Designers and Illustrators
Picture research by Tracy Cummins
Originated by Capstone Global Library Limited
Printed and bound in China by Leo Paper Group

16 15 14 13
10 9 8 7 6 5 4 3 2

Library of Congress Cataloging-in-Publication Data
Gallagher, Brigid.
 Langston Hughes / Brigid Gallagher.
  p. cm.—(American biographies)
 Includes bibliographical references and index.
 ISBN 978-1-4329-6455-9—ISBN 978-1-4329-6466-5 (pbk.) 1. Hughes, Langston, 1902-1967—Juvenile literature. 2. Poets, American—20th century—Biography—Juvenile literature. 3. African American poets—Biography—Juvenile literature. I. Title.
 PS3515.U274Z6425 2013
 818'.5209—dc23   2011037580
 [B]

Acknowledgments
The author and publishers are grateful to the following for permission to reproduce copyright material: AP Photo: pp. 9, 16, 35 (Matt Moyer), 38 (Bebeto Matthews), 40 (USPS); Corbis: pp. 8 (© CORBIS), 23 (© Underwood & Underwood), 31 (© Oscar White), 32, 37 (© St. Petersburg Times), 39 (© Ralf-Finn Hestoft); Getty Images: pp. 5 (Robert W. Kelley/Time & Life Pictures), 20 (Frank Driggs Collection), 28 (Fred Stein Archive/Archive Photos), 33 (Anthony Barboz), 41 (Fred Stein Archive/Archive Photos); Library of Congress Prints & Photographs Division: pp. 7, 11, 17, 21; Yale Collection of American Literature, Beinecke Rare Book and Manuscript Library: pp. 6, 10, 12, 18 ("Book Cover" copyright 1926 by Alfred A. Knopf, a division of Random House, Inc., from THE WEARY BLUES by Langston Hughes. Used by permission of Alfred A. Knopf, a division of Random House, Inc.), 19, 25 (Carl Van Vechten), 27 (Don Hunstein).

Cover photograph of Langston Hughes reproduced with permission from Getty Images (Hulton Archive).

Every effort has been made to contact copyright holders of material reproduced in this book. Any omissions will be rectified in subsequent printings if notice is given to the publisher.

Contents

Some words are shown in bold, **like this**.
These words are explained in the glossary.

A Great American Poet

What is your favorite book? Do you like reading and writing? Langston Hughes liked both as a child, and he turned out to be one of the greatest U.S. poets of all time. But he wasn't just a poet. He wrote plays, novels, short stories, and articles as well. Hughes began his career in the 1920s in Harlem, a neighborhood in New York City. He wrote until his death in 1967.

Spoken but not heard

Even though there were many African American poets before Hughes, they were hardly acknowledged. Very few people knew about African American authors because **racism** was an ongoing problem in the early 1900s in the United States. At the time, popular poems and books only told about the experiences of white people.

But this all changed during the **Harlem Renaissance**. This was a period during the 1920s and 1930s when African Americans began expressing their artistic and **intellectual** creativity. One of the strongest voices during this movement was that of Langston Hughes.

The voice of the people

In his writings, Hughes wrote about the lives of working-class African Americans. One of his favorite **themes** to write about was that "black is beautiful." During a time when many people treated African Americans poorly because of their **race**, this was a powerful message.

This photo shows Langston Hughes in front of his home in Harlem in 1958.

Early Childhood

James Mercer Langston Hughes was born in Joplin, Missouri, on February 1, 1902. His parents, Carrie Mercer and James Nathaniel Hughes, separated when he was very young. Hughes's father moved to Cuba, and later to Mexico. His mother was a schoolteacher and often traveled for work. Hughes was mainly raised by his grandmother, Mary Patterson Langston, in Lawrence, Kansas.

Langston is shown here with his mother, Carrie, in 1902.

The family storyteller

Hughes's grandmother loved to tell stories, and Hughes loved to listen to them. She told him funny stories and serious stories. Sometimes she told him about brave slaves who fought for freedom, like his **ancestors**. Other times she told him stories that made him laugh, because she had a great sense of humor.

Later in his life, Hughes gave his grandmother credit for helping him to discover his love of stories and books at an early age. She helped him to be proud of who he was and where he came from. Also, she taught Hughes the importance of getting an education. She was one of the first women to attend Oberlin College, in Oberlin, Ohio.

Did you know?

Some of Hughes's family members played important roles in history. In 1888 his great-uncle, John Mercer Langston, became the first African American to be elected to the United States Congress from Virginia. Hughes's grandfather, Charles Henry Langston, worked to end **slavery**. He was one of the leaders of the Ohio Anti-Slavery Society in 1858.

Hughes's great-uncle, John Mercer Langston, spent his life fighting for the rights of African Americans.

Paul Laurence Dunbar greatly influenced Hughes, as well as many other writers.

The bookworm

After Hughes's grandmother passed away in 1912, he went to live with family friends James and Mary Reed. Two years later, he moved with his mother to Lincoln, Illinois, where he attended grammar school.

During this time, Hughes was lonely. He was one of two African American students in his class. To escape his loneliness, he read books and wrote poetry. He discovered the work of writer Paul Laurence Dunbar. Dunbar was the first African American to receive national praise for his poetry. Hughes was very **inspired** by Dunbar's poems.

Did you know?

Hughes had ancestors from many different backgrounds. His great-grandmothers were African American. One of his great-grandfathers was Scottish, and the other was Jewish. His grandmother was African American, French, English, and American Indian. As a result, Hughes was African American, European American, and American Indian.

The class poet

Hughes graduated from eighth grade in 1916. At his graduation, he was elected class poet. But Hughes did not think he won the title because of his talent as a writer. He later said that in grammar school, his English teacher always talked about how important rhythm, or beat, was in poetry. Hughes felt that he had been **stereotyped**. He thought that because many people believed that black people had good rhythm, he won the title simply because he was black.

Langston is shown here in Lawrence, Kansas, where he lived with his grandmother.

The writer emerges

Hughes spent his high school years in Cleveland, Ohio. He went to Central High School, and his love for literature continued to grow. He was especially influenced by writers such as Walt Whitman and Carl Sandburg (see box). Hughes loved their poetic style. Studying their poems helped Hughes to shape his own poetic style. Whitman is known as the "father of **free verse**," which is a style of poetry that does not have a rhyming pattern. Whitman is one of the most important U.S. poets.

Langston Hughes is shown here in Cleveland, Ohio.

"When Sue Wears Red"

While in high school, Hughes wrote for the school newspaper, edited the yearbook, and began to write his first short stories, poems, and plays. He started to develop his own style of poetry, which was later named "**jazz** poetry."

Hughes is known as one of the founders of this form of poetry. Jazz poetry has the rhythm and style of **blues** and jazz music. In fact, jazz poetry often sounds like a song. Today, hip-hop music is a form of jazz poetry. Hughes wrote his first jazz poem, "When Sue Wears Red," while he was still in high school.

Carl Sandburg

(1878–1967)

Carl Sandburg was a U.S. poet and three-time winner of the Pulitzer Prize. The Pulitzer Prize is a special achievement award given to excellent writers, artists, and musicians each year. Like Walt Whitman, Carl Sandburg wrote free verse poetry. Hughes called Sandburg his "guiding star," because he was so influenced by Sandburg's poetry.

Many of Sandburg's poems are set in Chicago, where he worked as a reporter.

Young Adulthood

After Hughes graduated from high school, he decided to travel to Mexico to visit his father. He stayed there for a little over a year, returning to the United States in 1921.

Hughes's poem "The Negro Speaks of Rivers" was published before he went to college.

Did you know?

Hughes took a train from Cleveland, Ohio, to Mexico to live with his father for a short while. On the ride southwest to Mexico, he wrote one of his most famous and important poems, "The Negro Speaks of Rivers." Hughes was looking out the window as the train crossed over the Mississippi River, and he began to think about **slavery**. He thought about how so many slaves were sold down rivers throughout history. In Africa they were sold down the Euphrates, Congo, and Nile rivers. Before the Civil War (1861–1865) in the United States, slaves were sold down the Mississippi River. Hughes's poem was **published** in 1921 in *The Crisis*, the magazine of the National Association for the Advancement of Colored People (NAACP).

Off to college

Hughes went to New York City to attend Columbia University. Hughes's father paid for him to go to college, but only because Hughes promised to study engineering. His father did not support the young boy's desire to become a writer. Still, this did not stop Hughes from writing.

Hughes left Columbia University after one year, even though he got good grades. During his time at Columbia, Hughes discovered Harlem, a mainly black neighborhood in New York City. He spent a lot of time walking the streets, listening to live music, and meeting new people. All of these experiences influenced Hughes's writing, and they finally led him to his decision to leave Columbia.

World traveler

After Hughes left Columbia University, he took a job as a crewman, or sailor, on the S.S. *Malone*. He saw this as an opportunity to see the world. Hughes was on the ship for six months.

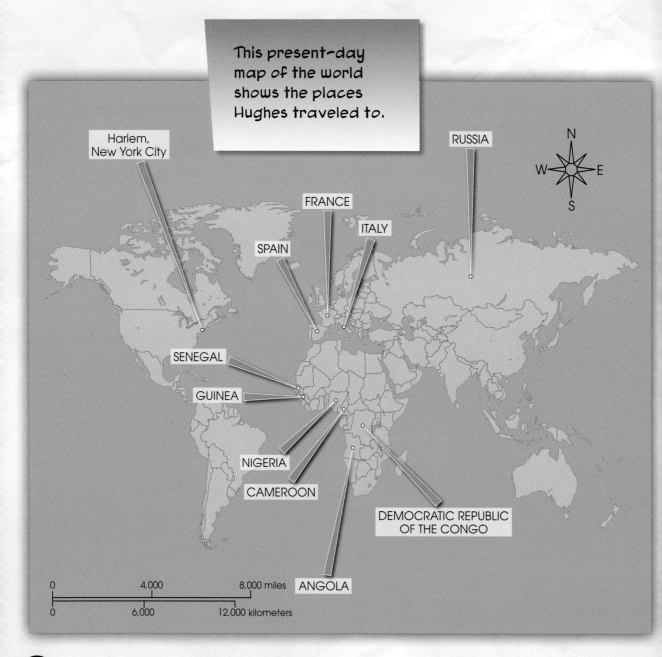

This present-day map of the world shows the places Hughes traveled to.

Harlem, New York City

RUSSIA

FRANCE

ITALY

SPAIN

SENEGAL

GUINEA

NIGERIA

CAMEROON

DEMOCRATIC REPUBLIC OF THE CONGO

ANGOLA

0   4,000   8,000 miles

0   6,000   12,000 kilometers

During his time traveling, Hughes saw many places in West Africa. He went to Senegal, Nigeria, the Cameroons (parts of present-day Cameroon and Nigeria), the Belgian Congo (present-day Democratic Republic of the Congo), Angola, and French Guinea (present-day Guinea). After this, Hughes traveled to Italy, Russia, and Spain. He spent six months working as a **busboy** in Paris, France, before returning to the United States in 1924.

Did you know?

Hughes wrote about the things that he saw and learned about other **cultures** during his travels. While Hughes was in Africa, he met a child who had one black parent and one white parent. Hughes noticed that both the black and white people in the village ignored the child. The way the community treated the child upset Hughes.

It is believed that his experience became a source of **inspiration** for a play that Hughes wrote in the early 1930s entitled *Mulatto: A Play of the Deep South*. The play was first performed on Broadway in New York City in 1935. It set a record for the number of performances and viewers for a play by an African American writer.

A Writer Is Discovered

In October 1924, Hughes moved to Washington, D.C., to be with his mother and her new husband. Hughes got a job as a personal assistant for Carter G. Woodson, who was a historian (person who studies history) at the Association for the Study of African American Life and History. Woodson is known as the "father of black history."

While he respected Woodson very much, Hughes was not happy with his job because it took time away from his writing. So Hughes quit and took a job as a **busboy** at the Wardman Park Hotel.

Carter G. Woodson is known as the "father of black history."

Hughes's big break

One day, while he was working at the hotel, Hughes saw
the poet Vachel Lindsay (see box) eating alone. As he was
clearing plates away from the table, Hughes placed a stack of
his poems in front of Lindsay. Lindsay read Hughes's poems.
He was so impressed by them that he got Hughes in contact
with Alfred A. Knopf, a **publishing** company in New York.
Lindsay also publicly announced that he had discovered a
new black poet: Langston Hughes.

Vachel Lindsay

(1879-1931)

Vachel Lindsay was a U.S.
poet. He is known as the
"father of modern singing
poetry." Singing poetry is
exactly what it sounds like:
poems that are meant to be
sung or chanted. Lindsay
often wrote about life in the
Midwest in his poems.

Vachel Lindsay
was a big fan of
Hughes's poetry.
Lindsay helped
Hughes to get his
poetry published.

First recognition

Knopf Publishing liked Hughes's poems as much as Lindsay did. In 1926 Knopf published Hughes's first book of poetry, *The Weary Blues*. The poem that he named the book after, "The Weary Blues," won Hughes his first poetry award. It was named best poem of the year by the magazine *Opportunity*. To this day, the poem is acknowledged as one of Hughes's greatest.

The Weary Blues was first published in 1926.

College graduate

The same year *The Weary Blues* was published, Hughes started college at Lincoln University in Chester County, Pennsylvania. Lincoln was the first African American university. Thurgood Marshall, who later became the first African American to serve on the United States Supreme Court (the highest U.S. court), was a classmate of Hughes's.

Throughout college Hughes continued to write. His second book of poems, *Fine Clothes to the Jew*, was published in 1927. In 1929 Hughes graduated from Lincoln University with a bachelor of arts degree. By that time, he had become well-known as a talented young writer.

Hughes was proud to graduate from Lincoln University, the first African American university in the United States.

Did you know?

At first many critics did not like Hughes's work. Most African American critics thought that Hughes wrote too much about problems within the black community. Hughes's writing often focused on lower-class African American life, and many people found it upsetting. In 1926 Hughes responded to his critics in his essay "The Negro Artist and the **Racial** Mountain." He argued that his poems were about racial pride and poetic freedom.

Harlem

After graduating from Lincoln University, Hughes moved back to Harlem in New York City. Aside from some traveling, Hughes would live in Harlem for the rest of his life.

Night clubs such as the Cotton Club were great places to listen and dance to jazz during the **Harlem Renaissance.**

Aside from literature and music, Hughes also appreciated art.

The blues and jazz music

One of Hughes's favorite things to do in Harlem was to sit in clubs and listen to **blues** and **jazz** music. He would write while he was listening to the music. Hughes loved blues and jazz because he felt that they expressed African American life.

Most of the songs Hughes heard dealt with people working hard to overcome difficulties. Some songs were sad and others were hopeful. Through his love of music, Hughes developed his own musical rhythm in his poetry. He wrote in his **autobiography**: "I tried to write poems like the songs they sang on Seventh Street." He said he did so because the songs "had the pulse beat of the people who keep on going."

More achievements

In 1930 Hughes **published** his first novel, *Not Without Laughter*. He was awarded the Harmon Gold Medal for Literature. His first collection of short stories, *The Ways of White Folks*, was published in 1934 and 1935. Hughes was also awarded the Guggenheim Fellowship, which is an impressive honor. The same year, his first play, *Mulatto* (see page 15), opened on Broadway in New York City.

The Harlem Renaissance

The Harlem Renaissance was a movement among African American artists that began around 1920 and ended around the mid-1930s. After World War I (1914–1918) ended, hundreds of thousands of African Americans living in the South moved north to big cities such as New York, Chicago, and Philadelphia. Many came to Harlem to write poetry and stories and create music and art that reflected the life of African Americans. The Harlem Renaissance allowed African Americans to celebrate their **culture** with pride, openly, for the first time. It was a very **inspiring** environment.

Harlem's writers, musicians, and artists

During the short period of time that the Harlem Renaissance blossomed, many great leaders, writers, artists, and musicians were discovered. Besides Hughes, other famous writers included Zora Neale Hurston, W. E. B. DuBois, and Countee Cullen. While their writing styles differed, writers during this period believed that by telling stories based on their personal experiences, they could change people's attitudes about **racism** and unite African Americans.

This map shows where Harlem lies within the island of Manhattan in New York City.

Brilliant musicians such as Louis Armstrong, Bessie Smith, and Duke Ellington created new sounds, moods, and feelings through their songs. Artists including Archibald Motley, Palmer Hayden, and Augusta Savage captured the spirit of the movement in their paintings and sculptures. All of these writers, musicians, and artists changed the way people viewed African Americans. Their impact can still be seen today.

Harlem in the 1920s was a very creative and inspiring environment for many people, including writers, musicians, and artists.

More Than Just a Poet

Hughes is most famous as a poet, but he was interested in more than just poetry. Like many of his peers during the **Harlem Renaissance**, Hughes believed that art could change the world. For Hughes, art was a way to help end **inequalities** and **prejudices**. It was a way to express his feelings about politics and fight for **civil rights**, or equal rights for all Americans, regardless of issues like **race**.

Did you know?

Throughout his life, Hughes traveled to other countries to learn about how they dealt with prejudice and issues related to race. He went to Spain in 1937, during the Spanish Civil War (1936–1939), to write articles on what was happening for the *Baltimore Afro-American* newspaper. It is said that while Hughes was there he met Ernest Hemingway, another famous U.S. writer, and they attended bullfights together.

Hughes fought for civil rights all throughout his life.

The children's writer

Hughes also wrote poetry and stories for children. As a young child, his grandmother's stories had **inspired** him to read and learn about history (see pages 6–7). So Hughes believed that writing for children was important. It was a way to introduce young people to new worlds and new ways of thinking.

Hughes cowrote his first children's book, *Popo and Fifina*, with his best friend, Arna Bontemps, in 1932. The story is about a Haitian family and their adventures moving from their home in the hills to a new town by the sea. It describes what life was like in Haiti at the time. After *Popo and Fifina*, Hughes went on to **publish** a dozen more children's books on topics such as Africa, the **West Indies**, animals, and **jazz**.

Did you know?

In the front of Hughes's home in Harlem, next to the stairs to his door, there was a small patch of land. No flowers or bushes grew there because the neighborhood children would run around on it, kicking up dirt. Hughes decided to make it a children's garden. He let each child in the neighborhood pick a plant that they were responsible for planting, watering, and weeding. The children's names were posted on a pole next to the plants. Hughes enjoyed spending time in the garden with the children, teaching them how to care for their plants.

Some of the children
from Hughes's garden
project are shown
here with him in 1955.

Hughes enjoyed writing plays and operas.

The playwright

Another one of Hughes's interests was the theater. He loved to write plays and **operas**. He wrote his first play, *Mule Bone*, with Zora Neale Hurston in 1930, but a disagreement between the two of them kept it from the stage. He also wrote many plays that were performed on Broadway and in other theaters, including *Little Ham* in 1936 and *Simply Heaven* in 1957.

Besides writing plays, operas, and lyrics (words) for musicals, Hughes also founded numerous theater groups throughout the country. In 1938 he started the Harlem Suitcase Theater in New York City. In 1939 he founded the New Negro Theater in Los Angeles, California. And in 1942 he started the Skyloft Players Theater in Chicago. Hughes's passion for the theater inspired other writers and gave actors opportunities to fulfill their dreams.

Jesse B. Simple

In 1942 Hughes began writing a weekly column (regularly printed series of writings) in the newspaper the *Chicago Defender*. He wrote the column for 20 years. Hughes often wrote it in the voice of a character he created, Jesse B. Semple, or Simple. The character was an everyday African American man who offered his opinion on current issues. Simple commented on numerous issues, but the topic he discussed most was **racism**. Audiences loved the character of Jesse B. Simple. He was very popular, so Hughes created a series of books about Simple, beginning in 1950 with *Simple Speaks His Mind*. Hughes's Jesse B. Simple books were turned into the musical *Simply Heaven*.

Influencing Others

People of all **races** were **inspired** by Hughes's work. Through his **themes** of **equality**, humor, and acceptance, Hughes encouraged other artists to write, sing, paint, and laugh. Just as Hughes was influenced by other art forms, such as **jazz**, his work inspired artists in other kinds of art as well.

Hughes wrote many, many volumes of poetry, novels, and stories for children and adults throughout his life. The chart below lists most of his major works.

The Weary Blues	poetry	1926
"The Negro Artist and the Racial Mountain"	essay	1926
Fine Clothes to the Jew	poetry	1927
Not Without Laughter	novel	1930
Mule Bone, with Zora Neale Hurston	play	1930
Dear Lovely Death	poetry	1931
The Negro Mother and Other Dramatic Recitations	poetry	1931
Scottsboro Limited	poetry & play	1932
The Dream Keeper and Other Poems	poetry	1932
Popo and Fifina, with Arna Bontemps	children's book	1932
The Ways of White Folks	short stories	1934
Mulatto	play	1935
Emperor of Haiti	play	1936
Little Ham	play	1936
Don't You Want to be Free?	play	1938
Let America Be America Again	poetry	1938
Troubled Island, with William Grant Still	play	1939
The Big Sea	nonfiction	1940
Shakespeare in Harlem	poetry	1942
Freedom's Plow	poetry	1943
Fields of Wonder	poetry	1947
One-Way Ticket	poetry	1949
Simple Speaks His Mind	short stories	1950
Montage of a Dream Deferred	poetry	1951

The First Book of Negroes	children's book	1952
Laughing to Keep from Crying	short stories	1952
Simple Takes a Wife	short stories	1953
Famous American Negroes	nonfiction	1954
The First Book of Jazz	children's book	1954
The First Book of Rhythms	children's book	1954
The First Book of the West Indies	children's book	1956
A Pictorial History of the Negro in America with Milton Meltzer	nonfiction	1956
I Wonder as I Wander	nonfiction	1956
Tambourines to Glory	play	1956
Simple Stakes a Claim	short stories	1957
Simply Heavenly	play	1957
Famous Negro Heroes of America	nonfiction	1958
Tambourines to Glory	novel	1958
The First Book of Africa	children's book	1960
Ask Your Mama: 12 Moods for Jazz	poetry	1961
The Best of Simple	comic	1961
Black Nativity	play	1961
Fight for Freedom: The Story of the NAACP	nonfiction	1962
Five Plays	plays	1963
Something in Common and Other Stories	short stories	1963
Jericho-Jim Crow	play	1964

Carl Van Vechten loved to photograph his friend, Langston Hughes.

Carl Van Vechten

(1880–1964)

Photography played an important role in Hughes's life. Carl Van Vechten was a U.S. poet and photographer who was good friends with Hughes. He took numerous photographs of Hughes, as well as other important people from the **Harlem Renaissance**, throughout their careers. Van Vechten also supported Hughes's work during his early years, which helped Hughes to become more popular.

The teacher

Hughes's talent and fame resulted in various colleges and universities asking him to teach literature classes. Most of the time, he rejected these job offers. He was too busy writing. However, in 1947 he accepted a position as a visiting professor of Creative Writing at Atlanta University. Two years later, in 1949, Hughes spent three months at University of Chicago Laboratory Schools as a visiting lecturer.

Hughes spent a few years as a college professor.

An inspiration to many

Hughes inspired many people outside of the classroom as well. For example, the title of playwright Lorraine Hansberry's play *A Raisin in the Sun* (1959) was taken from Hughes's poem "A Dream Deferred." Hansberry claimed that the poem was one of the **inspirations** behind the play, which was later turned into a movie and then into an award-winning Broadway musical. Novelist and poet Alice Walker (see box) has also often referred to Hughes as one of her greatest influences.

Alice Walker

(born 1944)

Hughes declared that he discovered writer Alice Walker, and she has acknowledged that Hughes helped guide her as a writer. She even wrote a book about him, entitled *Langston Hughes: American Poet*. Her most famous novel, *The Color Purple*, won the Pulitzer Prize for Fiction in 1983 and was later made into a movie. Walker continues to write books, short stories, poetry, and articles.

Alice Walker is one of many writers who were inspired by Hughes.

Langston's Legacy

Hughes continued to **publish** works until his death. He died in New York City on May 22, 1967, from problems after surgery he had as a result of **prostate cancer**. Hughes's body was **cremated**.

Did you know?

Throughout his lifetime Hughes received a number of important awards.

- In 1941 Hughes received the Rosenwald Fellowship, which is an award given to talented African Americans.
- In 1943 Lincoln University gave Hughes an honorary **doctorate** degree.
- In 1947 Hughes was elected to the American Academy of Arts and Letters.
- In 1961 the National Institute of Art and Letters elected Hughes as a member.

To hold Hughes's remains, the Arthur Schomburg Center for Research in Black **Culture**, a branch of the New York Public Library in Harlem, created the Langston Hughes Auditorium. Under the floor of this auditorium, Hughes's ashes were laid to rest.

Fact VS. Fiction

Later in his career, Hughes started to be known as the "Black Poet Laureate." Poet laureate is a special title given to writers who are officially selected by a government because of their exceptional talents. In Hughes's case, this was in fact just a nickname—there was not really such an official title in the United States. Still, it reflected how deeply Hughes was respected.

On the floor above the location of Hughes's ashes is a **cosmogram**. At the center of the cosmogram is a quote from Hughes's famous poem, "The Negro Speaks of Rivers": "My soul has grown deep like the rivers." Many people visit the site to pay their respects to Hughes.

Hughes's ashes are buried beneath this cosmogram.

Gone but not forgotten

Hughes has been described as the "most **prolific** and the most successful" of black writers during the **Harlem Renaissance** and beyond. In his lifetime Hughes wrote hundreds of poems, several poetry collections, novels and short stories, nonfiction books, major plays, and works for children. Hughes also wrote **operas**, essays, and articles, and he edited and translated other works.

There were many poems, plays, and children's books that Hughes wrote during his lifetime that were never published. Since his death, many of those works have been published. These include *The Panther and the Lash: Poems of Our Times.*

A number of biographies have been written about Hughes. Multiple essays about the importance of his work have been published. Hughes's plays continue to be produced on stage.

Did you know?

Hughes's influence has spread around the world. Many of Hughes's books have been translated into different languages, including German, Russian, Spanish, French, Yiddish, and Czech.

Hughes's papers

The Beinecke Rare Book and Manuscript Library is located at Yale University in New Haven, Connecticut. It holds the Langston Hughes Papers and the Langston Hughes Collection. The library contains letters, manuscripts, personal items, photographs, clippings, artworks, and objects that document the life of Hughes. Lincoln University also holds many of Hughes's papers in the Langston Hughes Memorial Library on campus.

This actor rehearses her part in Langston Hughes's play *Black Nativity: A Gospel Song Play.*

Hughes's home in Harlem is now a National Historic place and New York City landmark.

Langston Hughes Place

Since his death, people have looked for new ways to honor and remember Hughes. His home in Harlem has become an important symbol of his life. It is located at 20 East 127th Street. The street was given the honorary name Langston Hughes Place. In 1982 Hughes's home was listed on the National Register of Historic Places. It is also a New York City landmark. People come from all over the world to see Hughes's home.

Forever appreciated

People continue to honor Hughes by naming awards, schools, streets, and libraries after him. The following are just some of these honors:

- In 1973 the City College of New York created an award in Hughes's honor, known as the Langston Hughes Medal.
- In 1979 Langston Hughes Middle School was built in Reston, Virginia. Since then, multiple schools throughout the United States have been named after Hughes.
- In 1981 the Langston Hughes Society was created to carry on Hughes's legacy and recognize other talented **scholars**.
- There is a Langston Hughes Family Museum in Charlestown, Indiana.
- A Langston Hughes African American Film Festival is held each year in Seattle, Washington.

Several schools, including this one in Chicago, have been named after Langston Hughes.

"Hold fast to dreams"

Langston Hughes's poetry, short stories, novels, plays, essays, and articles are all filled with **themes** of struggle, joy, music, determination, hope, and laughter. Hughes wrote about what he knew. He wrote about the places where he lived and traveled. He wrote about himself, his beliefs, and the people he met throughout his life. And he wrote about issues and events that were important to him and—more importantly—to the culture of the United States.

It was everyday people who **inspired** Hughes. It was the fight for justice for all that encouraged him to continue writing. And it was his love for his community that filled him with passion. Hughes dreamed of becoming a writer from the time he was a child. His life is a success story.

Did you know?

On February 1, 2002, the U.S. Postal Service created a collectible postage stamp for its Black Heritage commemorative stamps series. The 34-cent Langston Hughes stamp paid tribute to one of the country's greatest African American leaders and artists. The importance of Hughes's life and work continues to be recognized today.

Hughes continued to write various works until his death in 1967.

Timeline

1902

Langston Hughes is born in Joplin, Missouri.

1909

The National Association for the Advancement of Colored People (NAACP) is founded.

1916

Hughes graduates from eighth grade.

1918

The Harlem Renaissance begins.

1924

Vachel Lindsay discovers Hughes.

1923

Hughes gets a job aboard the S.S. *Malone*.

1921

Hughes's poem "The Negro Speaks of Rivers" is published in *The Crisis*.

1920

Hughes graduates from high school.

1926

Hughes's first book of poems, *The Weary Blues*, is published.

1927

Hughes's second book of poems, *Fine Clothes to the Jew*, is published.

1929

Hughes graduates from Lincoln University.

1935

Hughes gets a Guggenheim Fellowship, and *The Mulatto* opens on Broadway.

1934

Hughes's first short story collection, *The Ways of White Folks*, is published.

1930

Hughes's first novel, *Not Without Laughter*, is published, and Hughes earns the Harmon Gold Medal for Literature.

1947

Hughes is elected to the American Academy of Arts and Letters.

1954

Hughes's *Simple Takes a Wife* is published and wins the Ainsfield-Wolf Book Award.

1960

Hughes receives the Spingarn Medal from the NAACP for outstanding achievement by an African American.

1982

Langston Hughes's Harlem home is listed on the National Register of Historic Places.

1981

The Langston Hughes Society is created.

1967

Hughes dies.

Family Tree

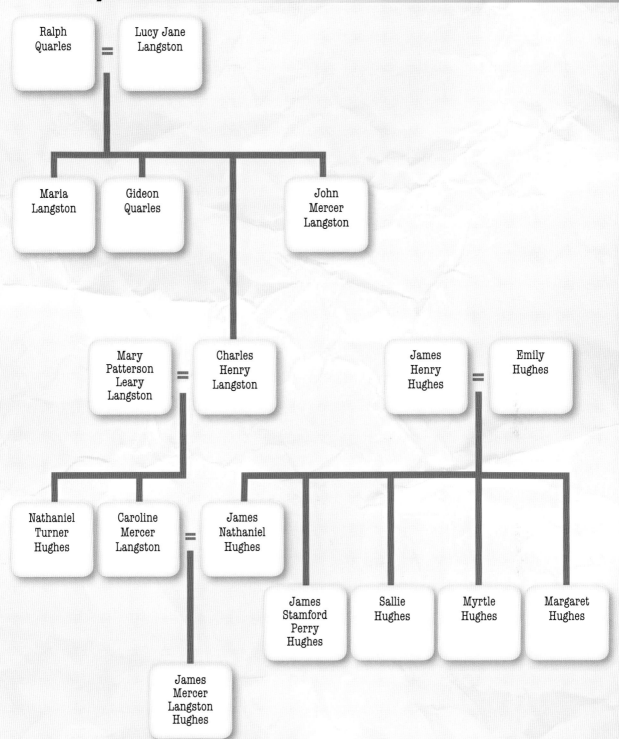

Ralph Quarles = Lucy Jane Langston

Maria Langston

Gideon Quarles

John Mercer Langston

Mary Patterson Leary Langston = Charles Henry Langston

James Henry Hughes = Emily Hughes

Nathaniel Turner Hughes

Caroline Mercer Langston = James Nathaniel Hughes

James Stamford Perry Hughes

Sallie Hughes

Myrtle Hughes

Margaret Hughes

James Mercer Langston Hughes

Glossary

ancestor person from whom one is descended; a relative who was born before you

autobiography nonfiction (true) book that a person writes about his or her life

blues type of music

busboy person who washes dishes, cleans tables, and does other jobs in a restaurant

civil rights equal rights for all Americans

cosmogram flat figure or image with a geometric pattern

cremate turn into ashes

culture shared beliefs, traditions, and behaviors belonging to a certain group of people

doctorate advanced, or high, degree awarded to a person who studies something for many years

equality belief that all people are equal and should have the same rights

free verse type of poetry that does not have a rhyming pattern

Harlem Renaissance African American cultural movement in the 1920s and 1930s in Harlem in New York City

inequality condition of being unequal, or treated as less than someone else

inspiration something that gives encouragement to do something

inspire to give someone encouragement to do something

intellectual relating to the mind and serious ideas; also a person dedicated to subjects of the mind and serious ideas

jazz type of music

opera type of play where the performance is sung, instead of spoken in a regular voice

prejudice dislike or hatred toward a person or group of people because of looks, background, beliefs, or any other characteristic

prolific producing a great amount or number of works or results

prostate cancer illness involving tumors, or abnormal growths, that affect part of the male reproductive system

publish prepare and print for public distribution or sale

race group of people who share similar characteristics such as skin color and whose distant relatives come from the same area

racial having to do with race

racism belief that race accounts for differences in human character or ability and that a particular race is superior to others

scholar person who attends school or studies with a teacher

slavery relationship in which one person has complete control over another person

stereotype regarding a person as embodying or conforming to a set image or type; an oversimplified idea, opinion, or image

theme topic or subject

West Indies islands of the Caribbean Sea

Find Out More

Books

Haskins, Jim, ed. *Black Stars of the Harlem Renaissance*. New York: John Wiley & Sons, 2002.

Hughes, Langston. *The Big Sea: An Autobiography*. New York: Hill and Wang, 1993.

Hughes, Langston. Arnold Rampersad, ed. *The Collected Poems of Langston Hughes*. New York: Vintage Classics, 1995.

Hughes, Langston. *The Sweet and Sour Animal Book*. New York: Oxford University Press, 1994.

Price, Sean Stewart. *Rebirth of a People: Harlem Renaissance*. Chicago: Raintree, 2007.

Roessel, David, and Arnold Rampersad, eds. *Poetry for Young People: Langston Hughes*. New York: Sterling, 2006.

Walker, Alice. *Langston Hughes: American Poet*. New York: Harper Collins Publishers, 2005.

DVDs

Hughes' Dream Harlem. Darralynn Hutson, 2002.
This film shows the viewer some of the places where Hughes liked to spend time in Harlem. It talks about how Hughes was able to successfully combine jazz, blues, and common speech in his work and explains why his work is still important today.

Voices & Visions: Langston Hughes. Winstar, 2000.
This interesting documentary includes interviews and recordings of Hughes reading and discussing his poetry. His friends are also included in this hour-long film about his life, work, and achievements.

Websites

American Academy of Poets
www.poets.org/poet.php/prmPID/83
This website includes a brief biography of Hughes and has the text of many of his poems. It also includes a few audio clips of him reading his poems.

Beinecke Rare Book and Manuscript Library, Yale University
http://beinecke.library.yale.edu/langstonhughes/web.html
This website has a large collection of Langston Hughes's papers, many of which are online. This is a great website to learn more about Hughes the writer and Hughes the person.

Poetry Foundation
www.poetryfoundation.org/bio/langston-hughes
This site includes a biography of Hughes, as well as poems, audio files, and essays.

Places to visit

"Rivers" Cosmogram
Arthur Schomburg Center for Research in Black Culture
515 Malcolm X Boulevard
New York, NY 10037
www.nypl.org/locations/schomburg

Langston Hughes's Home, New York City Landmark
20 East 127th Street
New York, NY 10035

Langston Hughes Memorial Library
Lincoln University
1570 Baltimore Pike
Lincoln University, PA 19352
www.lincoln.edu/library/

Index